"… if I have accomplished anything in life it is because I have been willing to work hard."

— Madam C. J. Walker

MADAM C. J. WALKER

By Lori Hobkirk

The Child's World®

GRAPHIC DESIGN
Robert E. Bonaker / Graphic Design & Consulting Co.

PROJECT COORDINATOR
James R. Rothaus / James R. Rothaus & Associates

EDITORIAL DIRECTION
Elizabeth Sirimarco Budd

COVER PHOTO
Portrait of Madam C. J. Walker
A'Lelia Bundles/Walker Family Collection
www.madamcjwalker.com

A very special thank you to Barbara Braswell and A'Lelia Perry Bundles.

Library of Congress Cataloging-in-Publication Data
Hobkirk, Lori.
Madam C. J. Walker / by Lori Hobkirk.
p. cm.
Includes index.
Summary: A biography of Sarah Breedlove Walker who, though
born in poverty, pioneered in hair and beauty care products
for black women and became a great financial success.
ISBN 1-56766-721-X

1. Walker, C. J., Madam, 1867-1919 — Juvenile literature.
2. Afro-American women executives — Biography — Juvenile
literature. 3. Cosmetics industry — United States — History —
Juvenile literature. 4. Women millionaires — United States —
Biography — Juvenile literature. 5. Afro-Americans —
Biography. 6. Cosmetics industry — History. [1. Walker, C. J.,
Madam, 1867-1919. 2. Businesswomen. 3. Afro-Americans —
Biography. 4. Women — Biography. 5. Cosmetics industry —
History.] I. Title.

HD9970.5.C672 W3544 2000   99-047008
338.7'66855'092 — dc21
[B]

Contents

Up the Mississippi

On December 23, 1867, the Breedlove family welcomed a new baby into their home. Her name was Sarah, and she was the youngest of three children. She was also the first person in her family who had not been born a slave.

It was the beginning of a new era. The American Civil War had ended two years earlier. **African American** slaves were finally free. But there was still a long, difficult road ahead for black people in the United States. Later in life, Sarah called herself Madam C. J. Walker. She changed her name to create a new life — for herself and for other African American women.

The Breedloves lived in the small village of Delta, Louisiana. It was close to the Mississippi River. After the war, they worked as **sharecroppers** on one of the smaller cotton plantations in the area. The land where they lived overlooked the Mississippi River. This powerful river was a symbol of freedom to many ex-slaves in the region. They believed it could transport them to a new and better life.

A'Lelia Bundles/Walker Family Collection

THE BREEDLOVE FAMILY'S SMALL CABIN IN DELTA, MISSISSIPPI.

©Bettmann/CORBIS

As riverboats traveled up and down the Mississippi, the river became a symbol of freedom for former slaves. They dreamed it could transport them to a new life.

©Bettmann/CORBIS

THIS FAMILY OF SHARECROPPERS LIVED IN A SMALL SHACK ON A PLANTATION, JUST AS THE BREEDLOVES DID. SHARECROPPERS WORKED HARD, BUT THEY EARNED VERY LITTLE MONEY.

Life for black children in the South was difficult. Sarah, her sister Louvenia, and her brother Alex worked all day in the cotton fields just as their parents did. The family also raised chickens and sold eggs. The children had no shoes to wear. Sarah's mother sewed new clothing for her family once a year. Each night, Sarah helped her mother and sister with the housework. They also did laundry for other families to earn extra money.

Like many black children in the South at the time, the Breedlove children could not go to school. They were too busy working on the farm. But even if there had been enough time, few black children had the chance to go to school. They could not attend the same schools as white children, and there were very few schools for blacks.

After working in the cotton fields all day, Sarah was tired. She often looked across the river to the town of Vicksburg, Mississippi. She longed for the "Promised Land" she heard people talk about. It was an unknown place where African Americans had the same opportunities other people had.

When she was seven years old, both of Sarah's parents became ill. At the time, there were many **epidemics.** Deadly diseases killed people throughout Louisiana. Former slaves were hit especially hard because they were so poor. They worked too hard and seldom had enough healthy food to eat. They could not go to the best doctors, who usually only treated white people.

Finally, yellow fever took the lives of Mr. and Mrs. Breedlove. Sarah, Louvenia, and Alex had to find a way to support themselves. Alex decided to cross the river and look for work in Vicksburg. When he did, Sarah and Louvenia's lives became even more difficult. They worked every waking hour just to have a little bit of food to eat.

Three years later, another epidemic of yellow fever spread throughout northeast Louisiana. It killed 3,000 people, most of whom were black. The cotton crop failed that year, too. Many people fled to Vicksburg, hoping to escape disease and poverty. But there was no promise of a better life in Vicksburg. Even so, the Breedlove girls moved across the river. Alex was still in Vicksburg, but not for long. Within two years, he married and moved to Denver, Colorado.

Sarah and Louvenia had never lived in a city before. So many poor people had fled to Vicksburg that jobs were difficult to find. Louvenia was lucky to find work as a washerwoman. She washed, ironed, and folded clothes. Sarah did whatever she could to help.

Louvenia married a man named Jesse Powell. Sarah and Jesse did not like each other. Powell was a cruel and angry man. Sarah longed to get away from him. She longed for the chance to go to school and to change her life. She dreamed of being the very best person she could be.

Sarah took the first step toward independence at age 14 when she married a man named Moses McWilliams. Three years later, she gave birth to her only child, a daughter named Lelia. Moses died in an accident not long after that. Some people believe he may have been the victim of a **lynching,** but no one knows for sure. Sarah did not talk about his death for the rest of her life.

Sarah was only 20 years old. She was a widow, and she had a young daughter to support. It was a difficult time. But she still refused to move back with Louvenia and Jesse.

Sarah continued to work hard. She hoped to find a way to leave Vicksburg. Finally, she earned enough money to buy two tickets on a riverboat. Sarah and Lelia were bound for St. Louis, Missouri, traveling up the Mississippi to a better life. Sarah was excited and afraid to move so far away. But she knew it was time for a change. Sarah believed she was on her way to the Promised Land.

©CORBIS

SARAH AND HER DAUGHTER TRAVELED UP THE MISSISSIPPI
UNTIL THEY ARRIVED AT THE ST. LOUIS PORT.

©Bettmann/CORBIS

MANY AFRICAN AMERICANS LEFT LOUISIANA AND MISSISSIPPI TO START A NEW LIFE IN ST. LOUIS. SOME WENT STRAIGHT FROM THE RIVERBOAT LANDING TO AFRICAN AMERICAN CHURCHES. THEY KNEW THE CHURCH MEMBERS WOULD HELP THEM GET STARTED.

Following a Dream

In 1888, Sarah and Lelia arrived in St. Louis. The city's size amazed them. More than 500,000 people lived there. More people arrived every day.

St. Louis was the gateway to the West. Wagon trains and pioneers bought supplies there. It also had one of the nation's largest black populations. About 35,000 African Americans lived in St. Louis.

Like Sarah, many southern African Americans came to St. Louis hoping to find a better life. Workers earned more money in St. Louis than in the South. There were also more jobs. Three St. Louis newspapers were published especially for blacks. African Americans also owned more than 100 businesses in the city.

Until Sarah moved to St. Louis, she was so busy working that she had little time to think about the future. She also had lost the people who were closest to her. Sarah knew it was important to form friendships in her new home.

When Sarah first arrived in St. Louis, she joined the St. Paul African Methodist Episcopal Church. The church was well known in the black community. Its members helped each other in many ways. Before the Civil War, Missouri had been a **slave state.** At the time, the church ran a secret school to teach African Americans to read and write. After the war, it helped former slaves find work, housing, clothing, and food.

The church members helped Sarah find work when she arrived in St. Louis. They also helped her find a place to live. Sarah now had two goals: to provide a good life for herself and her daughter, and to get an education for both of them. These seem like simple wishes. But in that day and age, even the most **prosperous** black communities faced many challenges. Employers paid black workers far less than they paid white workers. Sarah had to work 14 hours a day doing laundry. She worked at home so she could care for Lelia at the same time.

Once Sarah was settled, she wanted to help other African Americans. She was grateful for the church's generosity. Now she wanted to do something in return. She joined the church's Mite Missionary Society. This group helped people in need. Sarah offered a helping hand whenever she could. She raised money for an elderly black man and his blind daughter. She even organized a Southern-style **pound party** to stock their kitchen with food and other supplies. Helping people made Sarah feel good. She continued to do it for the rest of her life.

Lelia grew up during Sarah's years of hard work. Sarah saved money whenever she could. She planned to send Lelia to college. At the time, it was almost unheard of for an African American woman to go to college. But Sarah refused to think it could not be done. When the time came, Lelia moved to Tennessee to attend Knoxville College, a school for black students.

All of Sarah's effort and sacrifice did have its price. For one thing, she did not have much time to care for her appearance. She had been losing her hair for many years. Sarah had a medical condition called **alopecia.** Other black women had the same difficulty.

Many things contributed to alopecia. Black families often had little money. They could not always eat well. This prevented them from getting the proper nutrition for healthy hair. In addition, black people's hair is different from white people's hair. Most blacks have naturally short, curly hair, while white people often have straighter hair.

©CORBIS

St. Louis was a busy, bustling city when Sarah and Lelia arrived in 1888. It didn't take Sarah long to find work, especially with the help of her friends at St. Paul African Methodist Episcopal Church.

In the past, black women often lost their hair because they tried to wear it long, much as white women did. They used the same styling tools and products. This made their hair brittle and dry. Sometimes it broke off or even fell out altogether.

Sarah noticed that more prosperous women in the black community did not have this problem. They wore their hair pinned on top of their heads. Their hair was also smooth, long, shiny, and thick. How did they make their hair look that way? Sarah believed that if she could improve the way she looked, it might make her feel better about herself.

There were many hair-care products made especially for black women. Sarah tried all of them. Most contained chemicals that burned her **scalp** and caused even more hair to fall out. She tried to spread her hair on an ironing board and straighten it with an iron. That made it too dry and caused it to break.

White women also used metal hot combs to straighten their hair. But the combs' teeth were too close together for African American hair. Most women gave up, tied their hair in a scarf, and went back to work.

One night, Sarah tried to mix her own hair-growth **tonic.** She even prayed to God: If she could have a little help figuring out the correct ingredients, she would really appreciate it.

A'Lelia Bundles/Walker Family

SARAH WORKED SO HARD THAT SHE DIDN'T ALWAYS HAVE TIME TO TAKE CARE OF HERSELF. HER HAIR BEGAN TO FALL OUT BECAUSE OF A CONDITION CALLED ALOPECIA.

In a night of restless sleep, a black man came to Sarah in a dream. He whispered the names of special ingredients. He said they would help make her hair grow. She slept peacefully for the rest of the night. The next morning, Sarah prepared her new tonic. Soon, she would be selling it to African American women all across the United States.

Whenever people asked Sarah how she discovered her hair-growth recipe, she told that story. For most of her life, only two other people ever knew her exact recipe: her daughter Lelia, and a friend and coworker named Alice Kelly. Some people thought she ordered special **herbs** from Africa. Others thought her products included sulfur, a chemical used to treat skin diseases. Whatever ingredients Sarah used, her tonic worked.

At age 37, with Lelia in college, Sarah packed her bags. She moved to Denver, Colorado, to live with her brother Alex's family. Unfortunately, Alex had recently died. Sarah lived with his wife and four daughters. It was the beginning of a new life. Sarah's hair was growing back. She began to make plans to sell her tonic to other women around the country.

A'Leia Bundles/Walker Family

ALICE KELLY WAS A TEACHER IN KENTUCKY BEFORE SHE MET SARAH IN 1911. BY THAT TIME, SARAH HAD CHANGED HER NAME TO MADAM C. J. WALKER. SHE WAS ALSO SELLING HER HAIR-CARE PRODUCTS TO WOMEN AROUND THE COUNTRY. KELLY BECAME AN IMPORTANT FRIEND AND COWORKER TO MADAM WALKER. SHE WAS ONE OF THE ONLY PEOPLE WHO EVER KNEW THE HAIR-CARE TONIC'S SECRET INGREDIENTS.

SARAH MCWILLIAMS ARRIVED AT DENVER'S UNION STATION (CENTER) IN JULY 1905 WITH JUST $1.50 IN HER PURSE — ABOUT ONE WEEK'S PAY FOR WASHING LAUNDRY.

Western History/Geneology Dept., Denver Public Library

SARAH JOINED THE SHORTER AFRICAN METHODIST CHURCH AS SOON AS SHE ARRIVED IN DENVER. RELIGION WAS ALWAYS AN IMPORTANT PART OF HER LIFE.

On the Road

Sarah McWilliams liked Denver very much. Its bright blue skies were so different from the heavy, muggy air of St. Louis. There weren't as many African Americans living there, but the black community was growing. People's attitudes were also different. This was the West. It was a place of **expansion** and new ideas. Denver was a **boomtown.**

In the late 1800s, many Denver residents had struck gold in the Rocky Mountains. They used their wealth to build big houses and businesses. It was easier to find jobs in Denver than in St. Louis. It was also much easier for blacks to start a business. **Discrimination** against blacks still existed, but it wasn't as big a problem as it had been in St. Louis or the South.

Sarah continued to work hard. She did laundry two days a week. She also found part-time work at a drugstore. This job may have helped Sarah start her own business. A pharmacist named E. L. Scholtz owned the store. He probably helped Sarah perfect the recipes for her products.

Sarah enlisted the help of her sister-in-law and four nieces. They experimented with different formulas. Sarah wanted to make a good, **reliable** product. Within a few months, Sarah had created five hair-care products. They were designed to treat hair and the scalp in different ways.

Western History/Geneology Dept., Denver Public Library

CLERKS WAIT FOR CUSTOMERS TO ARRIVE AT E. L. SCHOLTZ'S PHARMACY IN DENVER. SARAH WORKED AT THE PHARMACY WHEN SHE FIRST CAME TO THE CITY. MR. SCHOLTZ MAY HAVE HELPED HER CHOOSE THE INGREDIENTS FOR HER PRODUCTS.

Sarah used the products on her own hair before she tried them on other people. First, she washed her hair using the "Vegetable Shampoo." It included **nutrients** that were missing from many black women's diets. Next, she used two other products, "Tetter **Salve**" and "Temple Grower." These treated burns and scratches from using other products or the hot comb. Then she applied "Wonderful Hair Grower," which was filled with vitamins and nutrients. Finally, she used "Glossine" hair oil with a heated steel comb. This treatment relaxed Sarah's tight curls. It also made her hair feel soft and healthy. Soon it began to grow thick and long.

Sarah decided to sell her products. She visited every house in her neighborhood. She used her own hair as an example of how well the hair-care products worked. When other women saw her lovely hair, they wanted to try them, too.

About that time, a man named Charles Joseph Walker came to Denver to visit Sarah. He was a friend from St. Louis. C. J., as everybody called him, decided to join her in Denver. It was a happy reunion for Sarah. They married in January 1906.

C. J. worked in the newspaper business. He had good ideas to share with Sarah. Together they devised a plan to sell the hair-care products. Sarah began calling herself Madam C. J. Walker. It was a smart move. Few black women used the fancy term "Madam." The name sounded important. Her new name stuck with Sarah for the rest of her life, even after she divorced C. J. in 1912.

Madam Walker believed that if women saw her beautiful head of hair, they would want to try her products. She also believed that she could sell more products if she dressed well. With a new name, a dark skirt, and a crisp white blouse, Madam Walker continued to sell her products door to door.

You cannot expect hair to grow and be healthy on a scalp that is unclean—a scalp covered with a parasite growth like dandruff. You wouldn't expect the flowers in your garden to grow fast and bloom profusely if choked by weeds, which also would sap the soil's nutrition to the detriment of the flowers. Thick, healthy hair can grow only on a scalp that is free from dandruff and scalp diseases.

BEFORE USING

Madam Walker before and after her wonderful discovery.

A'Lelia Bundles/Walker Family Collection

MADAM WALKER USED HER OWN IMAGE IN ADVERTISEMENTS FOR HER PRODUCTS. PHOTOS SHOWED WHAT HER HAIR LOOKED LIKE BEFORE AND AFTER USING HER HAIR-CARE SYSTEM. THE PRODUCTS MADE HER HAIR GROW HEALTHY AND LONG.

Madam Walker **demonstrated** her products in women's homes. She also advertised in African American newspapers across the country. An illustration of herself graced the packages of all her products. Her business began to grow. Women loved Madam C. J. Walker's Wonderful Hair Grower. It was her best-selling product.

Orders for Madam Walker's products came from across the country. She started a mail-order department so people could order and receive products through the mail. Lelia had recently graduated from Knoxville College. Madam Walker asked her to help with the new business.

Lelia was a wonderful addition to the company. At 21 years old, she stood a striking six feet tall. She was also very smart. At the time, not many African American women could boast a college education. Lelia carried herself with dignity and poise, qualities that Madam Walker found necessary to run a successful business.

Madam Walker's company began to make a profit of $10 per week. Such a salary was unheard of for black women at the time. She now earned four times what she once made doing laundry. She decided to use the company's profits to help her business grow. Her idea was to travel across the country selling her products.

A'Lelia Bundles/Walker Family Collection

MADAM C. J. WALKER'S VEGETABLE SHAMPOO WAS A POPULAR PRODUCT. IT CONTAINED SPECIAL NUTRIENTS TO MAKE HAIR HEALTHIER.

Madam Walker left Denver for a year and a half. She visited nine states throughout the North and South. She returned to her home state of Louisiana and made her way north to the exciting city of New York. Women were thrilled with her products. Madam Walker got an idea. If she hired some of her customers as salespeople, she could sell even more products. It was a brilliant idea. Madam Walker trained other women to demonstrate the hair-care products. In exchange, the salespeople received a **commission.** At the time, only the Avon company had sold beauty products door to door.

Madam Walker's company gave other black women new opportunities. They could become "hair culturists," as Madam Walker called her salespeople, instead of cooks or servants. Now she had more time to invent new products and to create interesting advertisements. The company profits grew to $35 a week. Not even many white men earned so much money.

The idea to recruit sales agents changed Madam Walker's business. In 1908, she and Lelia decided to move to the eastern United States. They chose Pittsburgh, Pennsylvania, as their new home. The Northeast had a large population of black people. From Pittsburgh, they could travel easily to other cities. Also, steel was manufactured in Pittsburgh. That was important for manufacturing Madam Walker's new steel comb.

Madam C. J. Walker's hair-care business blossomed in Pittsburgh. She opened a school where women were trained in the "Walker Method" of sales. The school was named Lelia College, after her daughter. **Tuition** for the program was $25. Madam Walker offered **scholarships** to those who could not afford the tuition. Women from all over the country came to Pittsburgh for instruction. Others learned through **correspondence courses.**

A'Lelia Bundles/Walker Family Collection

MADAM WALKER TRAVELED AROUND THE COUNTRY BY CAR FOR MORE THAN
A YEAR TO SELL HER PRODUCTS. ALONG THE WAY, SHE GOT AN IDEA: WHAT
IF HER CUSTOMERS HELPED HER SELL THE PRODUCTS TO OTHER PEOPLE?

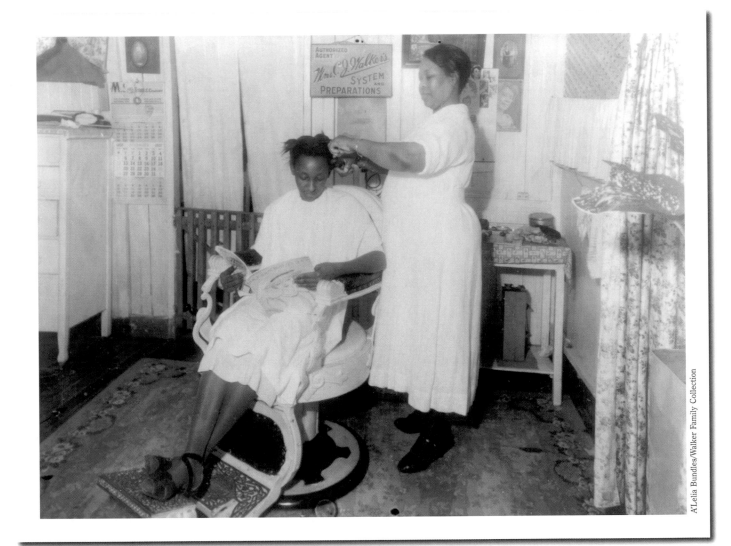

A'Leia Bundles/Walker Family Collection

A WALKER AGENT TENDS TO A CUSTOMER'S HAIR. MADAM WALKER
HELPED AFRICAN AMERICAN WOMEN FIND JOBS THEY ENJOYED AND
THAT MADE THEM FEEL GOOD ABOUT THEMSELVES.

Madam Walker settled in Pittsburgh for only two years. She was not content to slow down now that her company was successful. She wanted to make sure all black women heard about her products. She searched for another city with a large African American population. After many trips throughout the northern and southern United States, Madam Walker moved to Indianapolis, Indiana, in 1910. Indianapolis was located on the train route between New York, Chicago, and St. Louis. It was a good place to build a factory and to buy the supplies she needed to make her products.

Lelia — who had changed her name to A'Lelia — stayed in Pittsburgh. She ran Lelia College while Madam Walker continued to build her empire in Indianapolis. After one year in that city, her company employed nearly 1,000 "Walker Agents" across the country. Her factory employed another 3,000 people. Walker Agents sold and demonstrated the Walker hair-care system. They also opened their own Walker beauty salons across the country. Lelia College graduate Alice Kelly moved to Indianapolis to work at the factory. Madam Walker hired

her to be the factory's manager. Madam Walker always tried to employ women in her company's most important positions. Another valued assistant was Madam Walker's lawyer, F. B. Ransom. Madam Walker trusted Ransom with many of the important details of running a business.

A'Lelia Bundles/Walker Family Collection

F. B. Ransom became Madam Walker's general manager. He helped make important decisions for her successful company.

Sharing the Wealth

In six years, Madam C. J. Walker had gone from selling her products from door to door in Denver to employing 4,000 people nationwide. Her employees did more than just sell hair-care supplies. Many received an education from Lelia College. Some had earned scholarships. Many opened their own Walker beauty parlors in cities around the country.

Madam Walker's business was running well and earning an excellent profit. But she was not about to retire. From her childhood in Louisiana to her years in Indiana, Madam Walker never stopped working. In the last 14 years of her life, she ran a million-dollar business. She finally realized her dream of learning to read and write. She also learned how to drive. She traveled throughout the United States, Europe, West Africa, Central America, and the Caribbean. She became knowledgeable about literature, theater, and current events.

Money was not the most important thing in Madam Walker's life. She had always felt the need to help her people, and now she could use her business to do it. She was proud of what she had accomplished. Teaching African American women to care more about their appearance gave them confidence. It made them feel better about themselves. Perhaps most important, Madam Walker helped many blacks fulfill their own dreams of success and independence. Her company provided jobs — and self-respect — for thousands of black Americans.

In Indianapolis, Madam Walker hired African Americans to work in her factory. She had housing built for her employees. African Americans also built the housing where factory workers lived. She treated her employees with dignity and respect.

A'Lelia Bundles/Walker Family Collection

A NEW CLASS OF GRADUATES FROM MADAM WALKER'S SCHOOL,
READY TO START THEIR CAREERS AS HAIR CULTURISTS.

Madam Walker shared the money she earned. She donated $1,000 to the YMCA. She gave money to the National Association of Colored Women (NACW). She also donated money to schools dedicated to educating African Americans, such as the Tuskegee Institute and Bethune-Cookman College. She gave $5,000 to the National Association for the Advancement of Colored People (NAACP) to fight lynchings and **racism.** It was the largest donation the organization had ever received.

Throughout her life, Madam Walker continued to support the NAACP and other organizations. It pleased her to know that she could have a positive influence on the lives of others. Madam Walker wanted people to associate her company with generosity and goodness. Women who worked for Madam Walker were given awards for their good deeds. In 1916, she created the National Beauty Culturists and Benevolent Association of Madam C. J. Walker Agents. Each member paid 25 cents a month to a special fund. Then, when any member became sick or died, $50 was sent to that woman's family.

Of course, Madam Walker did enjoy the money she worked so hard to earn. In 1916, she began building the home of her dreams in Harlem, New York. Madam Walker called the mansion Villa Lewaro. In 1912, A'Lelia had adopted a young girl named Mae. Madam Walker asked them to live with her. She wanted her whole family to live together in the new home.

A'LELIA'S DAUGHTER, MAE. MADAM WALKER ASKED A'LELIA AND MAE TO LIVE WITH HER. SHE WANTED TO HAVE HER FAMILY CLOSE TO HER.

A'Leila Bundles/Walker Family Collection

MADAM WALKER BEAUTY CULTURISTS ATTENDED A CONVENTION AT VILLA LEWARO.
THE BEAUTIFUL MANSION SAT ON NEARLY FIVE ACRES ALONG THE HUDSON RIVER IN
NEW YORK CITY. THE NAME "LEWARO" WAS MADE UP OF THE FIRST TWO LETTERS
OF HER DAUGHTER'S THREE NAMES, LEILA WALKER ROBINSON.

Madam Walker only lived at Villa Lewaro for one year before she died. During that time, it was the center of many important events. Talented African American authors and artists came to Villa Lewaro. When she died on May 25, 1919, Madam Walker left the house to A'Lelia.

Madam Walker had asked that Villa Lewaro be given to the NAACP when A'Lelia died. The organization used the house as its national headquarters. Unfortunately, the NAACP had to sell the mansion during the **Great Depression** of the 1930s. It could not afford to take care of it. In 1976, Villa Lewaro was listed on the National Register of Historic Places.

Shortly before her death, Madam Walker summoned her assistant and lawyer, F. B. Ransom. Together they wrote $25,000 worth of checks to black charities and institutions. She still valued education. One donation included building a school for girls in West Africa.

After Madam Walker's death, F. B. Ransom and some of the Walker Agents ran the company. Many of Madam Walker's loyal employees continued to work for the company. It remained in business until 1985.

Madam Walker created a large, successful company all by herself. In 1918, she became the country's first female black millionaire. When she died a year later, more than 25,000 women were working for the company, which was earning $250,000 per year. But her true success cannot be measured in dollars.

Madam C. J. Walker believed that people are never truly successful unless they find a way to share their success. She taught other African American women how to feel good about themselves. She taught them to improve not only their appearance, but also their lives. Madam Walker proved to the nation that anyone with a goal can achieve something great.

A'Lelia Bundles/Walker Family collection

A'LELIA AT VILLA LEWARO. THE MANSION
BELONGED TO A'LELIA AFTER HER MOTHER
DIED. IT WAS DIFFICULT FOR HER TO LIVE
AT VILLA LEWARO BECAUSE SHE MISSED
HER MOTHER SO MUCH. SHE SPENT MOST
HER TIME AT A SMALLER HOUSE IN HARLEM.

Timeline

1867	Sarah Breedlove is born on December 23 in Delta, Louisiana.
1874	Sarah's parents die of yellow fever.
1878	Sarah and her sister, Louvenia, move to Vicksburg, Mississippi.
1882	Sarah marries Moses McWilliams.
1885	Sarah and Moses have a daughter, Lelia.
1887	Moses McWilliams dies. Sarah is 20 years old.
1888	Sarah and Lelia arrive in St. Louis, Missouri.
1904	Sarah has a dream in which a man tells her the names of secret ingredients for her hair-care products.
1905	Sarah moves to Denver, Colorado.
1906	Sarah Breedlove McWilliams marries Charles Joseph "C. J." Walker on January 4. She changes her name to "Madam C. J. Walker."
1908	Madam C. J. Walker moves to Pittsburgh, Pennsylvania, and opens Lelia College with her daughter.
1910	Madam Walker moves to Indianapolis, Indiana, to build a factory.
1912	The Walkers divorce. Madam Walker begins her trip around the country, selling products to African American women.
1913	Lelia, who has changed her name to A'Lelia, moves to Harlem, a section of New York City. She opens a second Lelia College and beauty salon.
1916	Madam Walker begins building her mansion, Villa Lewaro, in Harlem.
	Madam Walker begins the National Beauty Culturists and Benevolent Association of Madam C. J. Walker Agents.
1918	Madam Walker, A'Lelia, and Mae move into Villa Lewaro.
1919	Madam Walker dies on May 25 at age 51.

Glossary

African American (AF-ri-kun uh-MAYR-ih-kun)
African Americans are black Americans whose ancestors came from Africa. Madam C. J. Walker was an African American.

alopecia (a-loh-PEE-shuh)
Alopecia is a sudden loss of hair, or baldness. Madam C. J. Walker suffered from alopecia.

boomtown (BOOM-toun)
A boomtown is a town that has grown rapidly and has many jobs for people. Denver, Colorado, was a boomtown in the late 1800s.

commission (kuh-MIH-shun)
A commission is money paid to an employee for making a sale. Madam Walker's salespeople received commissions.

correspondence courses (kor-reh-SPON-dens KOR-sez)
Correspondence courses are classes taken by students who live far way from a school. Usually, the students send and receive class work through the mail.

demonstrated (DEH-mon-stray-ted)
Demonstrating a product is showing people how it works. The Walker Agents demonstrated hair products to African American women across the country.

discrimination (dis-krim-ih-NAY-shun)
Discrimination is unfair treatment of people (such as preventing them from getting jobs or going to school) because they are different. African Americans have suffered discrimination by whites.

epidemics (eh-pih-DEH-miks)
Epidemics occur when diseases spread rapidly through a group of people. Madam Walker's parents died during a yellow fever epidemic.

expansion (ek-SPAN-shun)
Expansion is an increase in the size of something. When Sarah arrived in Denver, the city was in a period of expansion.

Great Depression (GRAIT dee-PREH-shun)
The Great Depression was a period beginning in 1929 when business activity was very slow, and many people were out of work. Americans had very little money during the Great Depression.

herbs (ERBZ)
Herbs are plants that are used both to treat medical conditions and to spice food. Some people thought that Madam C. J. Walker used African herbs in her products.

lynching (LIN-ching)
A lynching is a murder by hanging that is carried out by a mob of people. Violent white gangs illegaly lynched at least 3,000 African Americans between 1880 and 1970 in the southern United States.

Glossary

nutrients (NEW-tree-entz)
Nutrients are substances that living things need for energy and growth. Madam Walker's products provided nutrients for hair.

pound party (POWND PAR-tee)
A pound party is a traditional Southern party, often given for newlyweds. Each guest brings a gift to the party that weighs no more than one pound.

prosperous (PRAH-spor-uss)
People who are prosperous are successful or fortunate. Even prosperous African Americans faced challenges during Madam Walker's lifetime.

racism (RAY-siz-im)
Racism is a negative feeling or opinion about people because of their race. Racism can be committed by individuals, large groups, or even governments.

reliable (ree-LY-uh-bul)
If something is reliable, it is worthy of trust. Madam Walker wanted her products to be reliable.

salve (SAAV)
A salve is a lotion that is put on sores and wounds. Madam Walker's "Tetter Salve" was used to treat burns and cuts on the scalp.

scalp (SKALP)
The scalp is the skin on the top and back of a person's head. The scalp is usually covered with hair.

scholarships (SKAHL-er-ships)
Scholarships are sums of money awarded to students to help pay for their education. Madam Walker offered scholarships to women who wanted to attend Lelia College.

sharecroppers (SHAIR-krop-erz)
Sharecroppers are farmers who work on another person's land. The landowner gives the farmers seed, tools, stock, living quarters, and food. The farmers receive part of the crop as payment.

slave state (SLAYV STAYT)
A slave state was an American state where slavery was legal. Missouri was a slave state before the Civil War.

tonic (TAHN-ik)
A tonic is a medicine that improves health or strength. Sarah Breedlove wanted to create a tonic for her hair.

tuition (too-IH-shen)
Tuition is a fee for attending school. Tuition at Lelia College was $25.

Index

Further Information

Books

Bundles, A'Lelia Perry. *Madam C. J. Walker.* Philadelphia: Chelsea House Publishers, 1991.

Grimes, Nikki. *Wild, Wild Hair (Hello Reader!).* New York: Cartwheel Books, 1997.

Haskins, James. *African American Entrepreneurs (Black Star Series).* New York: John Wiley & Sons, 1998.

Lommel, Cookie. *Madam C. J. Walker Entrepreneur.* Los Angeles: Melrose Square Publishing Company, 1993.

Web sites

Visit the Madam C. J. Walker home page, maintained by her great-great-granddaughter, A'Lelia Perry Bundles:
http://www.madamcjwalker.com

Visit Villa Lewaro on the Web:
http://www.madamcjwalker.org/villahist.htm

Learn more about Madam C. J. Walker:
http://www.lib.lsu.edu/lib/chem/display/walker.html

Learn more about life in the South for African Americans:
http://www.school.discovery.com/spring98/programs/tpl-anyplacebuthere/answers.html